BURLINGTON ZEPHYRS PHOTO ARCHIVE

AMERICA'S DISTINCTIVE TRAINS

John Kelly

Iconografix
Photo Archive Series

Iconografix
PO Box 446
Hudson, Wisconsin 54016 USA

Library of Congress Control Number: 2004102368

ISBN 1-58388-124-7

04 05 06 07 08 09 6 5 4 3 2 1

Printed in China

Cover and book design by Dan Perry

Copyediting by Jane Mausser

Cover photo-see page 82

BOOK PROPOSALS

Iconografix is a publishing company specializing in books for transportation enthusiasts. We publish in a number of different areas, including Automobiles, Auto Racing, Buses, Construction Equipment, Emergency Equipment, Farming Equipment, Railroads & Trucks. The Iconografix imprint is constantly growing and expanding into new subject areas.

Authors, editors, and knowledgeable enthusiasts in the field of transportation history are invited to contact the Editorial Department at Iconografix, Inc., PO Box 446, Hudson, WI 54016.

TABLE OF CONTENTS

Acknowledgments

This book is dedicated to my daughter Brenda Kelly, for her love and support through the years.

My sincere thanks to Suzanne Burris, Curator/Archivist for the Burlington Northern Santa Fe Railway, Fort Worth, Texas, for Burlington Zephyr archive photographs. To Kent Ohlfs, J. M. Gruber, Paul Knutson and Doug Wornom for their continuing friendship and for providing historic photographs for my books. Bill Raia and Bruce Meyer contributed Chicago area photos, and the Western History Collection of the Denver Public Library supplied Texas Zephyr material. Thanks also to the Iconografix staff for publishing this book.

During my research on the Burlington Zephyrs, I found many quotes and superlatives. In my opinion, E. F. Weber, a Burlington Superintendent, best summed the Zephyr experience in these words, "You would first notice a speck of stainless-steel emerging out of the distant haze. Then in spectacular fashion it would flash by, a mass of shimmering steel, traveling 100 miles an hour and within seconds vanish again in the distance."

On April 7, 1934, the shiny, three-car articulated train, Zephyr 9900 rolled out of the Budd Company's plant in Philadelphia. Its stainless-steel structure, diesel engine, sleek lines and streamlined design would have a profound influence on passenger trains in America for the next 30 years.

John Kelly
Madison, Wisconsin
January 31, 2004

INTRODUCTION

The Chicago, Burlington & Quincy (CB&Q), popularly known as the Burlington Route, suggests images of big-time railroading and the largest fleet of streamliners in the United States: the Burlington Zephyrs. The Zephyr idea originated in 1932 when Burlington President Ralph Budd noted declining passenger revenue on his railroad because of the Great Depression and the ascendance of automobiles and airplanes. He realized that something unique was needed to lure passengers back to train travel. Ralph Budd chose the name Zephyr for his new train after the "God of West Wind" in Greek mythology. On April 7, 1934, CB&Q introduced Zephyr 9900, built by the Budd Company (no relation to Ralph Budd) in Philadelphia. The train was assembled using Budd's "Shotweld" patented system of stainless all-steel construction. The rakish, shovelnose Zephyr 9900 and combination baggage–buffet–chair car 505, plus coach–parlor–observation car 570 were the vanguard of the Zephyr fleet. Burlington powered its ultramodern motor train with a Winton eight-cylinder 600-horsepower diesel engine. The aerodynamic, pocket streamliner was 197 feet long, carried 72 passengers, and was capable of speeds in excess of 100 mph.

On May 26, 1934, Burlington staged one of the greatest transportation events of the decade when Zephyr 9900 raced 1,015 miles in a record-breaking (13 hours 5 minutes) non-stop, dawn-to-dusk run at an average speed of 77.6 mph from Denver to Chicago's Century of Progress Transportation Fair. The Zephyr had set a world record for fast, long distance travel. Zephyr 9900 was later renamed Pioneer Zephyr and entered revenue service between Kansas City–Omaha–Lincoln on November 11, 1934. By the end of its first year of service, the Pioneer Zephyr had earned $95,000 in profits through increased ridership plus lower operating and maintenance costs compared to Burlington steam-powered trains. For CB&Q, the Pioneer Zephyr was the silver bullet that returned passengers to rail travel. By 1960, it had logged 3,222,898 miles when it was donated to Chicago's Museum of Science and Industry, where it is proudly displayed today. CB&Q management was so pleased with the success of the Pioneer Zephyr that soon fleets of Zephyr trains were added to the Burlington Route.

In 1935, one of the busiest passenger corridors in the Midwest was between Chicago and St. Paul–Minneapolis. It was here CB&Q chose to run its second and third Zephyr trains, in direct competition with Milwaukee Road's Hiawatha and Chicago & North Western's 400. The original, three-car Twin Zephyrs, 9901 and 9902, were inaugurated April 21, 1935. From Chicago Union Station, the Twin Zephyrs followed the Burlington commuter lines 38 miles west to Aurora, where the mainline diverged to Galesburg or Savanna, Illinois. From Savanna, it was a fast ride along the east bank of the Mississippi River to St. Paul, Minnesota. The Twin Zephyrs were so successful that CB&Q management recognized the need for bigger and better trains. In keeping with the Zephyr theme, locomotives and cars ordered for the second Twin Zephyrs, which premiered December 18, 1936, were again named after Greek mythology and known as "Train of the Gods and Goddesses." Led by locomotives 9904 Pegasus and 9905 Zephyrus, the car names included Apollo, Neptune, Mars, Vulcan, Mercury, Jupiter, Venus, Vesta, Minerva, Ceres, Diana, and Juno. The modern trains looked brilliant in silver and fluted stainless-steel finish. The name "Burlington" stood out in black sans serif lettering across the top letterboard of each car. Interior decor was art deco luxury with stainless-steel moldings, tubular lights, and pastel shades of blue, gray, and green. The sleek exterior design, including truck shrouds, of the updated Twin Zephyrs (later renamed Morning Zephyr and Afternoon Zephyr) contributed to the smooth, flowing streamlined style. The original Twin Zephyrs (9901 and 9902) eventually moved into service as the Sam Houston Zephyr (9901, Houston and Dallas–Ft. Worth), and Ozark State Zephyr (9902, Kansas City and St. Louis).

The Mark Twain Zephyr was the fourth Zephyr delivered to the CB&Q. Locomotive 9903 entered service October 28, 1935, from St. Louis, Missouri to Burlington, Iowa. The Mark Twain Zephyr was a four-car articulated train, similar in style to the original Twin Zephyrs. On May 31, 1936, CB&Q hastily transferred the Pioneer Zephyr and Mark Twain Zephyr to Chicago–Denver service. The trains were billed as Advance Denver Zephyrs, christened with new names, to beat Union Pacific's new City of Denver train, which was scheduled to begin service June 18, 1936. Meanwhile, the Budd Company was building new, overnight trains for the CB&Q, to be called Denver Zephyrs. The stainless-steel coaches and sleeping cars were not fully articulated into a single unit, but partially articulated in groups of three; the motive power was a separate unit. The larger, Denver Zephyrs required additional power, so CB&Q asked Electro-Motive Corporation in La Grange, Illinois, to design a shovelnose A-unit housing a pair of V-12 1,800-horsepower engines, coupled to a cabless booster B-unit, containing a single V-16 1,200-horsepower-rated engine. Both units rode on standard four-wheel trucks with a longer wheelbase. The Denver Zephyr locomotives were the first multiple-units on the Burlington roster. Beginning a CB&Q tradition, Denver Zephyr locomotives and cars were prefixed with the name Silver. Locomotive 9906A was "Silver King" and 9906B was "Silver Queen," while 9907A was "Silver Knight" and 9907B was "Silver Princess." On November 8, 1936, the trademark Burlington shovelnose locomotives were in vogue when they premiered as the Denver Zephyrs, on a fast 15-hour 50-minute, 1,034-mile overnight run from Chicago to Denver.

On April 20, 1939, the first non-articulated Zephyr made its debut with service between Kansas City and St. Louis, Missouri. The small, three-car train was named "General Pershing" Zephyr in honor of World War I General John Pershing. Shovelnose 9908, a combination locomotive–baggage car, was named "Silver Charger" after Pershing's horse. Locomotive 9908 was the most advanced of the shovelnose units and the last built. "Silver Charger" powered other Zephyr trains and remained on the Burlington roster until 1966, when it was donated to the St. Louis Museum of Transport for permanent display. The 11 shovelnose A–B units served the Burlington for 32 years, from 1934 to 1966. In 1940 and 1941, Burlington ordered 12 custom built diesels from Electro-Motive. Of these, nine were slant-nosed E5 cab units and three were booster units, all stainless steel to match the distinctive trains they intended to pull. Two of the last prewar additions to the Zephyr fleet were the Texas Zephyr (Denver–Dallas–Ft. Worth) in August 1940, and the Silver Streak Zephyr in April 1940. The Silver Streak replaced the original Pioneer Zephyr on the Kansas City–Omaha–Lincoln route. Another unique train was the Zephyr–Rocket, a partnership between Burlington and the Rock Island Railroad inaugurated in January 1941. The new train provided service from Minneapolis to Burlington, Iowa (via Rock Island) and from Burlington, Iowa, to St. Louis, Missouri (via Burlington Route).

In 1945, the innovative CB&Q introduced glass-topped Vista-Dome coaches. The first dome coach was built in Burlington's Aurora Shops and named "Silver Dome." The new dome car proved so popular that Burlington, in cooperation with Denver & Rio Grande Western, and Western Pacific, had 53 of them built by the Budd Company. The Vista-Domes debuted December 19, 1947, on the third and final set of Twin Zephyrs. The dome cars offered Burlington passengers' dramatic views of the upper Mississippi Valley's natural beauty. CB&Q route guides touted cliff-high palisades and abundant wildlife as the Mississippi River Scenic Line, "Where nature smiles 300 miles." The Twin Zephyrs were the first streamliners in the United States to feature regularly scheduled dome cars. These new trains were rated the finest in the Zephyr fleet and they were fast. The sleek trains sped the distance between Chicago and the Twin Cities in 6 hours 45 minutes. For many years, the Morning Zephyr–Train 21 had the fastest overall running time in the world, 84 mph between East Dubuque, Illinois, and Prairie du Chien, Wisconsin. Burlington was also a forwarder of passenger traffic for parent Hill Lines (Great Northern/Northern Pacific) in the busy Chicago–Twin Cities corridor. In later years, Great Northern's Empire Builder and Northern Pacific's North Coast Limited were often combined with the Twin Zephyrs on the St. Paul–Chicago portion of their transcontinental runs. Both flagship trains looked superb behind pairs of CB&Q silver E-units.

During the postwar years (1945 to 1947), the entire Zephyr fleet was upgraded with new or refurbished equipment. The first postwar Zephyr was the Nebraska Zephyr, introduced November 16, 1947, between Chicago–Omaha–Lincoln, replacing the Ak-Sar-Ben (Nebraska spelled backwards) Zephyr. Burlington had a banner year in 1953 with the introduction of two new Zephyr trains: on February 1, 1953, the Kansas City Zephyr and American Royal Zephyr (overnight train) premiered between Chicago–Kansas City–St. Joseph, Missouri; in October 1956, Burlington built the final trains in the Zephyr fleet, the Vista-Dome Denver Zephyrs. At that time, the Denver Zephyrs were considered the finest overnight trains in America.

To many travelers the California Zephyr was the grandest passenger train of all. These superb Budd-built, stainless-steel trains began service March 20, 1949, between Chicago and San Francisco (Oakland) on the Burlington Route, the Denver & Rio Grande Western, and the Western Pacific. The California Zephyr route traversed some of the most spectacular scenery in the United States. Both westbound and eastbound trains were scheduled for scenic viewing during daylight hours, offering a captivating ride in Vista-Dome coaches. The trains followed Burlington trackage from Chicago to Denver, Colorado. Denver & Rio Grande Western handled the trains over the magnificent Front Range of the Colorado Rockies from Denver to Salt Lake City, Utah. Western Pacific then took the trains from Salt Lake City through California's awesome Feather River Canyon and into Oakland. For many passengers, dining on the California Zephyr was a memorable experience, with real china, linen, fresh flowers, and regional cuisine. Each of the six California Zephyr trainsets had an on-board Zephyrette hostess, who handled passenger dinner reservations, first-aid, announcements, and public relations. Despite Burlington's investment in passenger trains, the late 1950s and 1960s were unkind to all passenger trains. By 1970, declining passenger revenue (due to automobiles and jet airliners) ended the California Zephyr's 21-year reign. The most talked-about train in the country had taken its place in railroad history.

Not to be forgotten, though, was the tremendous appeal of the original Pioneer Zephyr, whose sleek lines and streamlined design signaled the beginning of a styling revolution. In 1934 Depression days, the only real hope was the future and the future was the Zephyr. The new train increased revenues and provided hope for both the railroad and the American public that times would improve. The silver streamliner proved what could be done when the will to succeed and creative imagination were combined. During the peak years of passenger rail, the Zephyr was more than just transportation: it was the modern way to travel. Burlington kept up that image as it maintained far-reaching passenger service to Chicago, Denver, Dallas–Ft. Worth, Houston, St. Louis, Kansas City, Omaha, Oakland, and the Twin Cities with its fleet of Burlington Zephyrs, America's Distinctive Trains.

CHAPTER 1- PIONEER ZEPHYR: BUILT OF STAINLESS STEEL

Ralph Budd, President of the Chicago, Burlington & Quincy Railroad posed in the cab of streamlined Zephyr 9900, circa 1934. *Courtesy Burlington Northern Santa Fe Railway*

Chicago, Burlington & Quincy publicity photo of Budd-built, streamlined Zephyr 9900 in 1934. *Courtesy Burlington Northern Santa Fe Railway*

Curious crowds gathered during the promotional tour of Burlington Zephyr 9900. The new train combined the best of stainless all-steel construction and art deco design. Date and location unknown. *J. M. Gruber collection*

The Zephyr Dawn–to–Dusk Club with "Zeph" the mascot burro. Photographed in Chicago, May 26, 1935, after the Burlington Zephyr 9900's historic 1,015-mile non-stop Denver to Chicago. *Harry Rhoads photo, Denver Public Library, Western History Collection*

May 27, 1934, Zephyr 9900 was on display at the Chicago Century of Progress Transportation Fair. Visitors lined up to tour Burlington's newest train. *Courtesy Burlington Northern Santa Fe Railway*

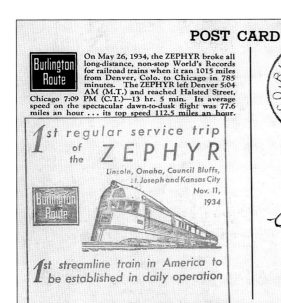

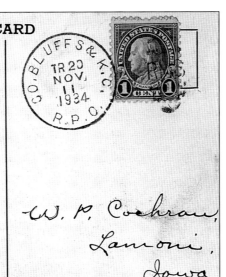

POST CARD

On May 26, 1934, the ZEPHYR broke all long-distance, non-stop World's Records for railroad trains when it ran 1015 miles from Denver, Colo. to Chicago in 785 minutes. The ZEPHYR left Denver 5:04 AM (M.T.) and reached Halsted Street, Chicago 7:09 PM (C.T.)—13 hr. 5 min. Its average speed on the spectacular dawn-to-dusk flight was 77.6 miles an hour ... its top speed 112.5 miles an hour.

Burlington Route

1st regular service trip of the ZEPHYR

Lincoln, Omaha, Council Bluffs, St. Joseph and Kansas City

Nov. 11, 1934

Burlington Route

1st streamline train in America to be established in daily operation

W. P. Cochran, Lamoni, Iowa,

Post card with Railway Post Office (RPO) date and stamp, November 11, 1934, to commemorate Zephyr 9900's first revenue trip between Lincoln, Omaha, and Kansas City. The "Wings to the Iron Horse" promotional brochure was for Burlington Zephyr 9900 and Chicago Century of Progress Transportation Fair, 1934. *Author's collection*

Wings to the Iron Horse

Burlington Pioneers Again ====►

Burlington

THE WEST WIND

Zephyr

First Diesel Streamline Train

The "Zephyr Pit" on Canal Street, south of Roosevelt Road in Chicago, where streamlined Zephyr motor trains were serviced. Date unknown. *J. M. Gruber collection*

The Pioneer Zephyr—Daddy of 'em All

FIRST DIESEL STREAMLINE TRAIN IN AMERICA

1934—TENTH ANNIVERSARY—1944

MORE THAN A TRAIN ... A SYMBOL

● Burlington's Pioneer Zephyr, first diesel-powered, streamline train in America ... symbol of a dramatic era in railroad transportation ... and of the even more dramatic progress to come.

Christened on April 18, 1934 ... exhibited in 222 cities in 27 states ... tested through 30,000 experimental miles, the Pioneer Zephyr entered regular service with national acclamation, on November 11, 1934 ... thus establishing the first streamline service in America.

Today, the Burlington has fourteen gleaming stainless steel Zephyrs operating on its system lines.

More than 100 trains, fashioned to the streamline pattern, have gone into service for railroads throughout the country.

With ten years of outstanding service to its credit—a period during which it has covered in excess of 1,676,000 miles—the Pioneer Zephyr is still on active duty, serving wartime America to the tune of 456 miles each day.

In the coming peacetime years, we look forward to a program of further improvement and refinement of the "streamline train" era, inaugurated by the Pioneer Zephyr ten years ago.

Way of the Zephyrs

Burlington Route

AN ESSENTIAL LINK IN TRANSCONTINENTAL TRANSPORTATION

National Geographic 10th anniversary (1944) advertisement for the Pioneer Zephyr. The name was changed from Zephyr 9900 to Pioneer Zephyr on November 11, 1936. *Author's collection*

Pioneer Zephyr in service at Omaha, Nebraska, May 9, 1938. Notice a fourth car had been added to the original three-car train for additional seating. *Bill Raia collection*

The Pioneer Zephyr is shown flying white flags to denote passenger extra at Longmont, Colorado. Date unknown. *J. M. Gruber collection*

Pioneer Zephyr running as Denver to Cheyenne–Train 31, arrived at Longmont, Colorado, on Burlington subsidiary Colorado & Southern Railway, October 1949. *J. M. Gruber collection*

Aeolus 4000 was the first stainless-steel streamlined steam locomotive to proudly display the Burlington Route herald. August 8, 1937, location unknown. *Grant Oaks photo, J. M. Gruber collection*

Burlington
Route

Rebuilt from S-4 class 4-6-4 locomotive in April 1937, Aeolus 4000 was used as the backup locomotive for the Twin Zephyrs and Denver Zephyr. *Grant Oaks photo, J. M. Gruber collection*

Aeolus 4000 led the Overnite Denverite at Princeton, Illinois, June 28, 1939. The train handled overflow passenger business from the Denver Zephyr. *Bill Raia collection*

Burlington Route public time-tables for October to December 1935 promoted four new Zephyr trains in Burlington's streamline fleet. *Author's collection*

BURLINGTON'S STREAMLINE FLEET

DIESEL POWERED • • • BUILT OF STAINLESS STEEL

THE FIRST ZEPHYR	THE TWIN ZEPHYRS	THE MARK TWAIN ZEPHYR
In regular daily service since November 11, 1934.	Twice daily service each way — 882 miles round trip.	Introduced in October, 1935.
LINCOLN OMAHA COUNCIL BLUFFS ST. JOSEPH KANSAS CITY	CHICAGO LA CROSSE ST. PAUL MINNEAPOLIS	ST. LOUIS HANNIBAL QUINCY BURLINGTON
Holder of the world's long distance non-stop record for railroad trains.	Over the Burlington's famed water-level route along the Upper Mississippi River.	Commemorating the 100th anniversary of Mark Twain, immortal author, raconteur, and steamboat pilot who lived and wrote in and of Hannibal, Missouri, on the Mississippi River.

The most illustrious train family in the world

Burlington's Aeolus was pulling the "Ak-Sar-Ben" Zephyr alongside the Twin Zephyr, November 8, 1937, at West Hinsdale, Illinois. *Courtesy Burlington Northern Santa Fe Railway*

Twin Zephyrs (9901 and 9902) posed for the company photographer on June 2, 1935, east of Aurora, Illinois. The sleek trains looked fast just standing still. *Courtesy Burlington Northern Santa Fe Railway*

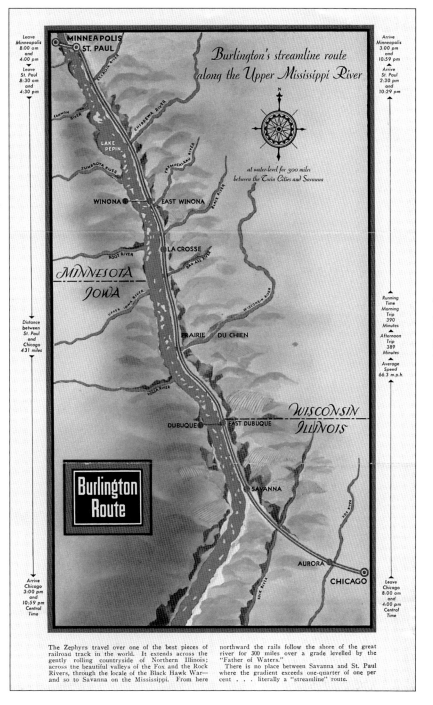

The Twin Zephyr map and travel brochure featured Burlington's streamline route along the Upper Mississippi River, circa 1938. *Author's collection*

Beginning December 20, 1936, Burlington 9902 (formerly Twin Zephyr) was assigned to St. Louis–Kansas City service as the Ozark State Zephyr (Trains 32, 33). Note the Alton-Burlington nose plate on locomotive 9902. The two railroads shared joint operation of the train from Kansas City to St. Louis, Missouri, May 1938. *Author's collection*

Zephyr 9902 near Princeton, Illinois, October 30, 1945. The train provided Chicago–Ottumwa, Iowa, service from August 1945 to May 1947. *Bill Raia collection*

After leaving the Budd Company plant in Philadelphia, the four-car Mark Twain Zephyr 9903 was displayed at various eastern cities. October 8, 1935, the train was at the Lehigh Valley Freight Station in Bethlehem, Pennsylvania. *J. M. Gruber collection*

Mark Twain Zephyr observation car "Tom Sawyer" on display at Bethlehem, Pennsylvania, October 8, 1935. Note the Mark Twain bronze plaque and replica signature on the rear of the car. *J. M. Gruber collection*

Mark Twain Zephyr 9903 (Trains 43, 44) with service from St. Louis, Missouri, to Burlington, Iowa, departed St. Louis on July 12, 1938, passing the Gratiot Street Tower and the Ralston Purina elevator. *Bill Raia collection*

The Mark Twain Zephyr map and travel brochure featured Burlington's route from St. Louis, Missouri, to Burlington, Iowa, circa 1936. *Author's collection*

Burlington transferred the Mark Twain Zephyr 9903 and Pioneer Zephyr to Chicago–Denver service on May 31, 1936. They were billed as the Advance Denver Zephyrs to compete with Union Pacific's City of Denver stream-liner. Photographed at Galesburg, Illinois, June 1, 1936. *Courtesy Grayland Station*

Denver Union Station, circa late 1960s. The station served the Denver Zephyr, Texas Zephyr, Union Pacific's City of Denver, and other fine passenger trains. Note the "Union Station—Travel by Train" sign and clock. *Denver Public Library, Western History Collection*

JANE GARLOW, GRANDDAUGHTER OF BUFFALO BILL
CHRISTENS THE NEW DENVER ZEPHYR
(RUNNING TIME: DENVER TO CHICAGO - 15 HRS. 50 MIN.)
SATURDAY EVENING, OCTOBER 24 AT DENVER, COLO.

Denver Zephyr christening ceremony, October 24, 1936, at Denver Union Station. Jane Garlow, granddaughter of Buffalo Bill Cody, broke the champagne bottle on Denver Zephyr locomotive 9906A "Silver King." *Courtesy Burlington Northern Santa Fe Railway*

Denver Zephyr locomotive 9907A "Silver Knight," at Denver Union Station. Date unknown. *J. M. Gruber collection*

Original Burlington Zephyrettes left to right; Marion Steele (Chicago), Marion and Mildred Haggerberger (twins from McCook, Nebraska), and Catherine Chapman (Chicago). The Zephyrette tradition dated from 1936 when Burlington put hostesses on the Denver Zephyr, and later on the Twin Zephyrs. Photographed at Chicago, Illinois, 1936. *Courtesy Burlington Northern Santa Fe Railway*

Travel brochure for the new 12-car Denver Zephyrs featured arrival and departure schedules, interior car views, and the slogan "America's Distinctive Trains." Circa 1936. *Author's collection*

The Denver Zephyr cocktail lounge car featured the latest in art deco streamline design with Formica tables and stainless-steel tubular chairs, November 8, 1936. *Courtesy Burlington Northern Santa Fe Railway*

The Denver Zephyr dining car waiter served first-class meals to passengers on tables set with white linen, real china, and fresh flowers, November 8, 1936. *Courtesy Burlington Northern Santa Fe Railway*

Passengers enjoyed the surroundings of the smartly decorated Denver Zephyr observation car "Silver Flash" on November 8, 1936. *Courtesy Burlington Northern Santa Fe Railway*

Exterior view of "Silver Flash" observation car shows the sleek stainless curved end with the Denver Zephyr moniker. Chicago, Illinois, 1936. *J. M. Gruber collection*

The "Zephyr Pit" diesel maintenance facility in Chicago had completed work on Denver Zephyr locomotive 9906A "Silver King" when this photo was taken in 1936. *J. M. Gruber collection*

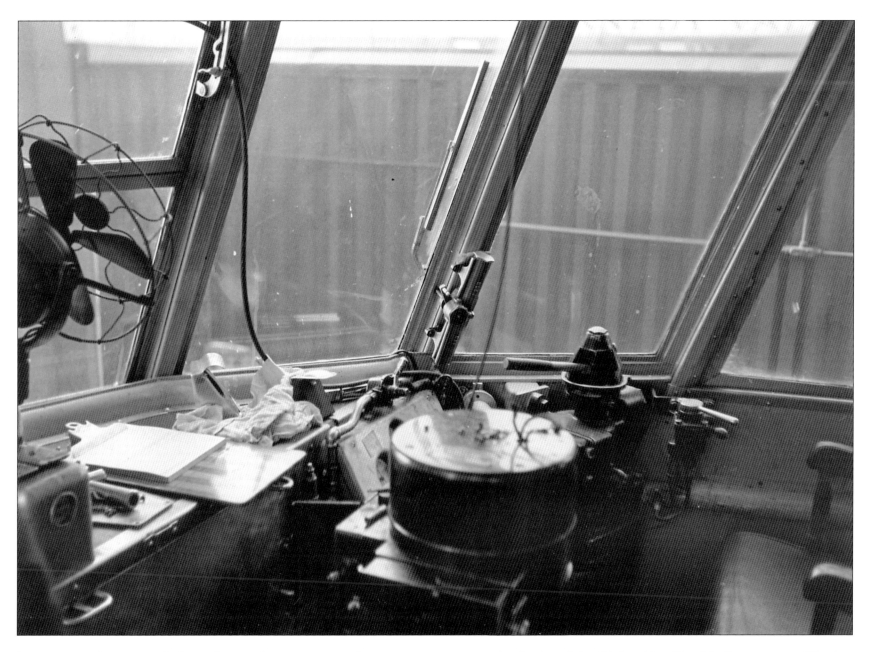

Interior cab view of shovelnose locomotive shows engineer control stand built by the Budd Company. Photographed at Chicago, Illinois, Date unknown. *J. M. Gruber collection*

Galesburg, Illinois, was an important stop on the Denver Zephyr schedule. The engineer on locomotive 9906A "Silver King" waited patiently for the conductor's "All Aboard" and the beginning of the eastbound run to Chicago Union Station. Date unknown. *J. M. Gruber collection*

Lincoln, Nebraska, was another station stop for the Denver Zephyrs. On April 17, 1949, locomotive 9906A "Silver King" had just arrived, while the Nebraska Zephyr was serviced on adjacent trackage. *Bill Raia collection*

The NEW 7-CAR TWIN Zephyrs

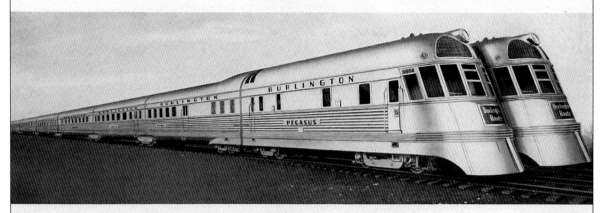

"AMERICA'S DISTINCTIVE TRAINS"

Morning and Afternoon between

CHICAGO — ST. PAUL — MINNEAPOLIS

To meet the popularity that overwhelmed the passenger capacity of its smaller Zephyrs, the Burlington created The New 7-Car Twin Zephyrs —a brilliant achievement in travel luxury.

These fine, new super-Zephyrs consolidate the smooth fleetness for which the Zephyrs are noted with broad new concepts of spaciousness, comfort and elegance.

Each of these New Twin Zephyrs is composed of an 1800-horsepower Diesel-electric power car; a smartly-styled cocktail lounge; two luxurious, fully-carpeted coaches seating 120 passengers; a beautiful dining car, and two richly-appointed parlor cars, one providing a spacious private drawing-room and the other a delightful observation-lounge.

Features of The New Twin Zephyrs include: coach and parlor car porters . . . train hostess . . . radio-phonograph outlets . . . arm-rests dividing coach seats fold out of way . . . wide, clear-vision windows . . . inter-car telephone system . . . cars wider than conventional equipment. Both coach and parlor car seats reserved and assigned by number in advance.

Ride one of these New Twin Zephyrs on your next trip between Chicago and the Twin Cities. Super-speed, super-comfort and super-luxury but NO EXCESS FARE.

THREE FINE NIGHT TRAINS DAILY

Black Hawk
Observation - lounge car, salon-bedroom car, matched Pullmans, de luxe reclining chair car. Buffet.

North Coast Limited
Observation-club car, matched Pullmans, tourist sleeping cars, dining car and de luxe coaches.

Empire Builder
Lounge - observation car, matched Pullmans, tourist sleeping cars, dining car and de luxe coaches.

All Trains Completely Air-Conditioned

Burlington Route travel brochure advertised the new seven-car Twin Zephyrs between Chicago–St. Paul–Minneapolis. Note the "America's Distinctive Trains" slogan, circa 1938. *Author's collection*

First official photograph of the new Twin Zephyr, December 15, 1936, eastbound to Chicago with 100 Twin Cities business and civic leaders aboard. *Courtesy Burlington Northern Santa Fe Railway*

Locomotive 9905 "Zephyrus" led the Twin Zephyr at Hastings, Minnesota, September 24, 1938. *Robert Graham photo, Kent Ohlfs collection*

The "General Pershing" Zephyr was named after World War I General John Pershing, and was the first non-articulated Zephyr to debut. Photographed April 20, 1939, departing St. Louis for Kansas City, Missouri. Note the joint operation Alton–Burlington nose plate on locomotive 9908. Date unknown. *J. M. Gruber collection*

Burlington locomotive 9908 was named after General Pershing's horse, "Silver Charger" and the cars were named for emblems of rank for commissioned Army officers: "Silver Star," "Silver Eagle" and "Silver Leaf." Photographed at Galesburg, Illinois, during the exhibition tour in 1939. *Courtesy Grayland Station*

"Silver Charger" was essentially a stainless-steel baggage car with a modern Electro-Motive diesel engine in the forward compartment. Photographed at Aurora, Illinois, on March 28, 1948. *J. M. Gruber collection*

"Silver Charger's" non-articulation allowed the locomotive to be interchanged on other Burlington passenger trains including older heavyweight cars. Shown departing St. Louis, Missouri, on August 4, 1956. *J. M. Gruber collection*

The "Silver Pendulum" was designed by Northrup Aircraft engineers and one of three built by Pacific Railway Equipment Company. This chair car tilted on curves and offered passengers an almost lurch-free ride. "Silver Pendulum" was delivered in 1942 and used on various Burlington trains. Photographed at Council Bluffs, Iowa, on June 20, 1957. *J. M. Gruber collection*

One of the last prewar additions to the Zephyr fleet was the Texas Zephyr, providing overnight service from Denver to Dallas–Ft. Worth, Texas, beginning August 22, 1940. From Denver, the train operated over Burlington subsidiary lines, Colorado & Southern Railway, and the Fort Worth and Denver Railway. The Colorado & Southern locomotive 9951-A was photographed at Denver Union Station, November 11, 1956. *Bill Raia collection*

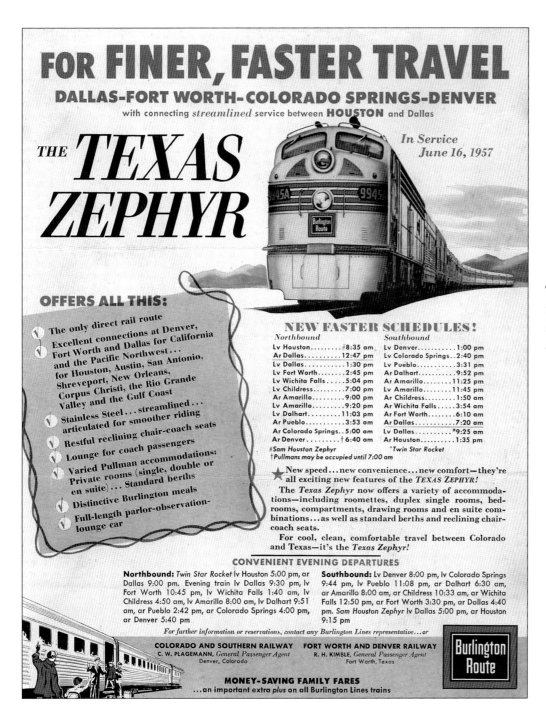

This Texas Zephyr travel brochure showed the train's northbound and southbound schedules plus other train information, circa 1957. *Author's collection*

Interior view of the Denver, Colorado, diesel service facility, photographed May 22, 1946. *J. M. Gruber collection*

This interior view of the Denver diesel service facility shows Forth Worth and Denver locomotive 9980-A, which powered the Texas Zephyr. *J. M. Gruber collection*

Colorado & Southern (Train 22), six-car Texas Zephyr, led by locomotive 9950-A "Silver Racer" arrived at Denver, Colorado, in 1965 during a snowstorm. *Otto Perry, Denver Public Library-Western History Collection*

Texas Zephyr, led by locomotive 9981-B, January 16, 1961, at Palmer Lake, Colorado. *J. M. Gruber collection*

Texas Zephyr locomotive 9950-A "Silver Racer" is shown at Pueblo, Colorado, June 9, 1964. Note the Santa Fe Railway locomotive 81 and heavyweight baggage car on adjacent track near the depot. *Bill Raia collection, courtesy Kent Ohlfs collection*

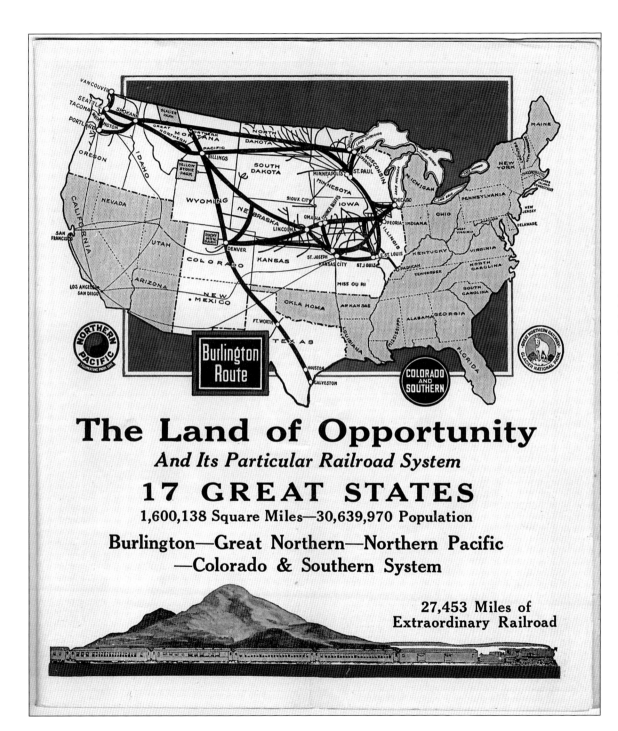

Burlington Route December 1922 to January 1923 public timetables displayed the system map for Burlington Route and partner railroads. *Author's collection*

The front cover of Burlington's 1955 foldout travel brochure featured the "Vista-Domes that re-vitalized train travel." *Kent Ohlfs collection*

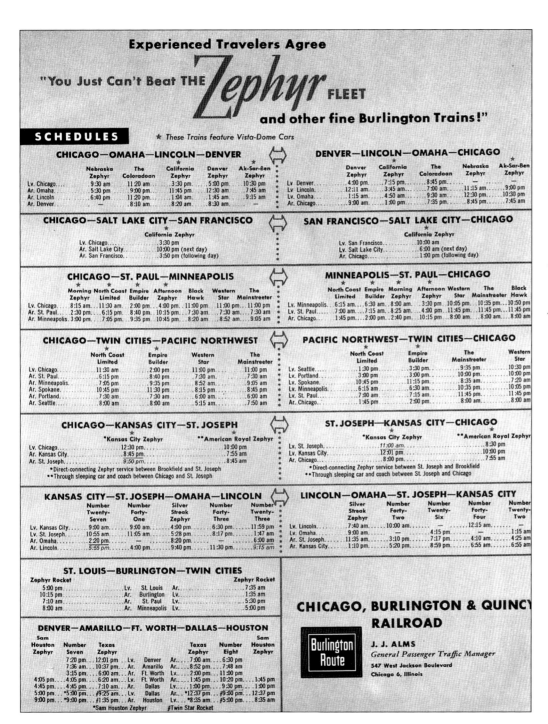

The back cover of Burlington's 1955 foldout travel brochure proclaimed, "You just can't beat the Zephyr fleet and other fine Burlington passenger trains." *Kent Ohlfs collection*

Burlington's first Vista-Dome coach was built in 1945 from chair car 4714 "Silver Alchemy" and renamed "Silver Dome." Chicago, Illinois, August 21, 1971. *Owen Leander photo, J. M. Gruber collection*

Burlington Vista-Dome parlor-observation car 361 "Silver Vista" served on many Zephyr trains. Note the open-rack automobiles on the St. Charles Air Line in the background. Chicago, Illinois, September 21, 1968. *Owen Leander photo, J. M. Gruber collection*

Burlington Vista-Dome coach 4720 "Silver Rifle" was built for California Zephyr service. Chicago, Illinois, July 5, 1970. *Owen Leander photo, J. M. Gruber collection*

Burlington Vista-Dome lounge-observation 378 "Silver Lookout" served on California Zephyr trains. Note the "Everywhere West" Burlington slogan on the Crooks Terminal Warehouse. Chicago, Illinois, May 31, 1968. *Owen Leander, photo. J. M. Gruber collection*

Mississippi River Scenic Line (1949) travel guide slogan for third set of Twin Zephyrs promoted "Where Nature Smiles Three Hundred Miles," in reference to the upper Mississippi River on one side, and high bluffs on the other side. *Author's collection*

Burlington Twin Zephyr with Vista-Domes provided passengers with lovely views along the upper Mississippi River route. St. Paul, Minnesota, June 19, 1947. *Bill Raia collection, courtesy Kent Ohlfs*

Burlington travel brochures touted "Three hundred miles of see-level scenery along the Father of Waters." Twin Zephyr with five Vista-Domes was featured in a July 1948 company publicity photo along the upper Mississippi River route. *Courtesy Burlington Northern Santa Fe Railway*

Savanna, Illinois, was a crew change for Burlington passenger train crews between Chicago, Illinois, and North La Crosse, Wisconsin. Note the engineer wearing traditional white cap, exiting locomotive 9994 with grip in hand. Date unknown. *Kent Ohlfs collection*

During the 1965 Mississippi River floods, Burlington trackage along the river line was washed out in many places. Burlington detoured trains over the Chicago & North Western and the Milwaukee Road from April 12 to April 28, 1965. Left to right; Milwaukee Road, Burlington Route, and Northern Pacific passenger trains at Milwaukee Road's Milwaukee, Wisconsin, depot. April 1965. *Bob's Photos*

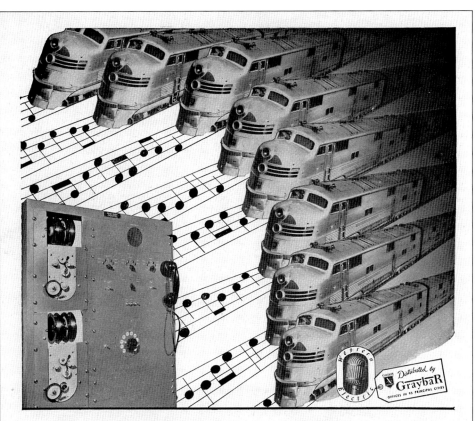

This advertisement for Western Electric Program Distribution Systems is from *Railway Age* magazine, circa 1949. *Author's collection*

Burlington provided motive power for both Great Northern and Northern Pacific passenger trains between Chicago and the Twin Cities. August 31, 1947, had Great Northern's Empire Builder at Rochelle, Illinois, led by Burlington locomotive 9917. *Bill Raia collection, courtesy Kent Ohlfs*

November 6, 1965, Great Northern's Empire Builder (westbound) derailed at Lee, Illinois. The entire train left the rails but the cars did not overturn. *Bill Raia collection, courtesy Kent Ohlfs*

Northern Pacific's North Coast Limited was photographed October 11, 1955 at Oregon, Illinois, led by Burlington locomotive 9967. *Bill Raia collection, courtesy Kent Ohlfs*

"Hello, I'm *Sue*, Your Stewardess-Nurse"

"Sue" exemplifies the corps of friendly, capable young women, all registered nurses, who help make travel more pleasurable on the

VISTA-DOME
NORTH COAST
LIMITED

One of the World's
Extra Fine Trains

F6917   PRINTED IN U S A

Northern Pacific 1963 travel brochure for the North Coast Limited illustrated the nurse-stewardess service aboard the train from Chicago to Seattle. *Author's collection*

The Nebraska Zephyr with articulated trainset was photographed east of Pearl Street in Galesburg, Illinois, headed to Chicago, August 28, 1948. *Bill Raia collection*

Burlington parlor-observation car 226 "Jupiter," originally built for the second set of Twin Zephyrs, was assigned to Nebraska Zephyr service in 1947. Chicago, Illinois, June 27, 1970. *Owen Leander photo, J. M. Gruber collection*

February 1, 1953, Burlington premiered the Kansas City Zephyr with daily service from Chicago to Kansas City. Train 35 is shown departing Chicago with two Vista-Dome cars, March 8, 1954. *Courtesy Burlington Northern Santa Fe Railway*

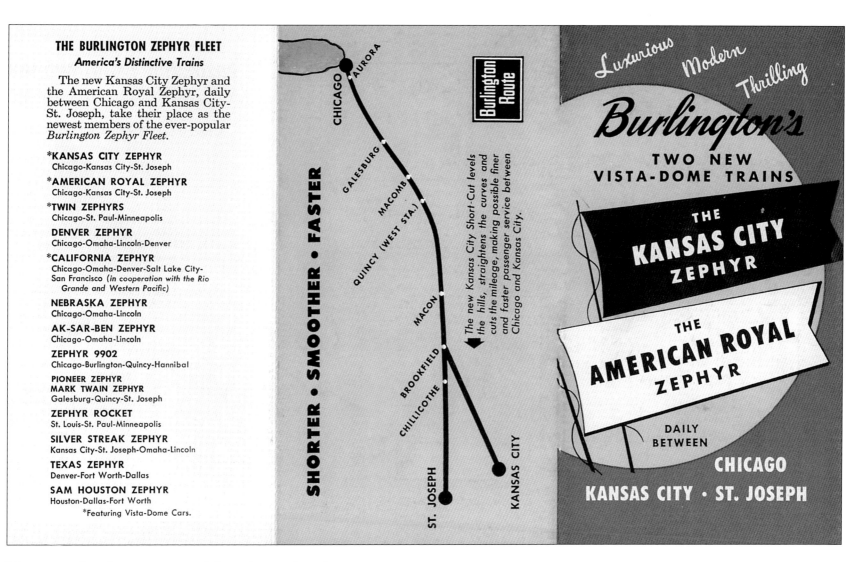

THE BURLINGTON ZEPHYR FLEET
America's Distinctive Trains

The new Kansas City Zephyr and the American Royal Zephyr, daily between Chicago and Kansas City-St. Joseph, take their place as the newest members of the ever-popular *Burlington Zephyr Fleet.*

*KANSAS CITY ZEPHYR
Chicago-Kansas City-St. Joseph

*AMERICAN ROYAL ZEPHYR
Chicago-Kansas City-St. Joseph

*TWIN ZEPHYRS
Chicago-St. Paul-Minneapolis

DENVER ZEPHYR
Chicago-Omaha-Lincoln-Denver

*CALIFORNIA ZEPHYR
Chicago-Omaha-Denver-Salt Lake City-San Francisco *(in cooperation with the Rio Grande and Western Pacific)*

NEBRASKA ZEPHYR
Chicago-Omaha-Lincoln

AK-SAR-BEN ZEPHYR
Chicago-Omaha-Lincoln

ZEPHYR 9902
Chicago-Burlington-Quincy-Hannibal

**PIONEER ZEPHYR
MARK TWAIN ZEPHYR**
Galesburg-Quincy-St. Joseph

ZEPHYR ROCKET
St. Louis-St. Paul-Minneapolis

SILVER STREAK ZEPHYR
Kansas City-St. Joseph-Omaha-Lincoln

TEXAS ZEPHYR
Denver-Fort Worth-Dallas

SAM HOUSTON ZEPHYR
Houston-Dallas-Fort Worth

*Featuring Vista-Dome Cars.

SHORTER • SMOOTHER • FASTER

CHICAGO
AURORA
GALESBURG
MACOMB
QUINCY (WEST STA.)
MACON
BROOKFIELD
CHILLICOTHE
ST. JOSEPH
KANSAS CITY

Burlington Route

The new Kansas City Short-Cut levels the hills, straightens the curves and cuts the mileage, making possible finer and faster passenger service between Chicago and Kansas City.

Luxurious Modern Thrilling

Burlington's
TWO NEW
VISTA-DOME TRAINS

THE
KANSAS CITY
ZEPHYR

THE
AMERICAN ROYAL
ZEPHYR

DAILY
BETWEEN
CHICAGO
KANSAS CITY • ST. JOSEPH

This is a Burlington travel brochure for the Kansas City Zephyr and American Royal Zephyr (overnight train) from Chicago to Kansas City, Missouri, circa 1954. *Author's collection*

Pioneer Zephyr and Kansas City Zephyr photographed together at Brookfield, Missouri, May 25, 1954. *J. M. Gruber collection*

Burlington premiered the second Denver Zephyrs with Vista-Domes, October 28, 1956. This train ranked as one of the finest overnight trains in the United States. *Courtesy Burlington Northern Santa Fe Railway*

The Vista-Dome Denver Zephyrs were the last of the Burlington Zephyrs to be built, and the last passenger train in America built by a private railroad. Burlington locomotive 9985B led the Denver Zephyr at Naperville, Illinois, May 25, 1964. *J. M. Gruber collection*

Burlington Alco yard engine 9307 switched the Denver Zephyr at Denver Union Station, July 21, 1963. *Kent Ohlfs collection*

Led by Burlington locomotive 9915B, the new Denver Zephyrs introduced Slumbercoaches (budget sleeping rooms), and the mid-train "Chuck Wagon" dome–dormitory–buffet lounge car. Photographed in Colorado on October 31, 1956. *J. M. Gruber collection*

The Denver Zephyr carried the blunt-end Vista-Dome parlor–buffet–observation car "Silver Chateau," complete with the Denver Zephyr tail-sign. Photographed in Colorado on October 31, 1956. *J. M. Gruber collection*

CHAPTER 4 - CALIFORNIA ZEPHYR: GRANDEST TRAIN OF ALL

"Look up, look down, look all around" proclaimed the advertisement for the most talked-about train in the country, the Vista-Dome California Zephyr. *National Geographic* advertisement, date unknown. *Author's collection*

The California Zephyr, America's favorite land-cruise train in the 1950s and 1960s, looked very sleek with Vista-Domes on exhibition tour at Peoria, Illinois, March 12, 1949. *Bill Raia collection*

In 1949, a Burlington 9960C F3 set rounded the curve at Naperville, Illinois, with the California Zephyr including five Vista-Dome cars. *Jay Williams collection*

To power the new California Zephyr, three unit F3 sets of locomotives numbered 9960-ABC, 9961-ABC, and 9962-ABC, all painted silver to match the equipment were added to the Burlington roster in 1947. These locomotives were equipped with steam boilers and traction motors geared for high-speed passenger service. Locomotive 9960C is shown with the California Zephyr at Galesburg, Illinois, August 23, 1949. *Bill Raia collection*

The Western Pacific Railroad was a partner in California Zephyr train operations, and owned Vista-Dome Observation car 881 "Silver Crescent." Note the Pennsylvania Railroad run-through sleeping car ahead of "Silver Crescent." August 23, 1966, Galesburg, Illinois. *Bill Raia collection*

The California Zephyr was designated as Train 17–westbound and Train 18–eastbound. On June 18, 1969, at Galesburg, Illinois, Burlington E8 9942B led the California Zephyr–Train 18 to Chicago. *J. M. Gruber collection*

The California Zephyr

Each of the California Zephyrs, in addition to Diesel locomotive and baggage-express car, regularly has the following cars in the order shown — all designed to afford the utmost in comfort and convenience:

Three Vista-Dome Chair Coaches
Nos. CZ 22, 21, 20

Each chair coach has 42 reserved reclining chairs on the "main floor," plus a family group of 4 chairs facing each other. All chairs, except the family group of four, have adjustable leg and foot rests. The Vista-Dome in each coach has 24 seats for the use of passengers holding reserved coach seats. All coaches are fully carpeted; have full-vision windows, restful fluorescent lighting and spacious washrooms.

Coach passengers may secure a downy-soft pillow from coach porter for 25¢ per night.

The Vista-Dome Buffet-Lounge Car

Inexpensive light meal and beverage service is available in this car. The Vista-Dome, seating 24, is for the use of sleeping car passengers only.

The Dining Car

Seats 48. Breakfasts as low as $1.10; luncheons from $1.60 up; select dinners from $1.85 up. Also a la carte service.

Sleeping Car—CZ 16

Six double bedrooms and five compartments. Each room has private lavatory; electrically-refrigerated drinking water; 110-volt outlet for electrical appliances; individual temperature control, radio and recorded-music; Venetian blinds; adjustable seats.

Sleeping Cars—CZ 15 and CZ 14

Each car has ten roomettes and six double bedrooms containing same refinements as the rooms in CZ 16, above.

Sleeping Car—CZ 12

Sixteen semi-private sections, the first two of which are 6 ft. 8 in. long, for tall travelers.

Sleeping Car—CZ 11

Between New York and San Francisco. Ten roomettes, six double bedrooms. Similar to CZ 15 and CZ 14.

Vista-Dome Observation-Lounge Car—CZ 10

The rear car, with lounging facilities for 50 sleeping car passengers, including 24 seats in the Vista-Dome, also has a drawing room (with private shower bath) and three double bedrooms.

The California Zephyr is not an extra fare train, but coach and Pullman space is reserved and assigned in advance. Seats in the Vista-Domes are NOT reserved, and may be occupied without any extra payment.

J. J. ALMS,
General Passenger Traffic Manager
Chicago, Burlington & Quincy Railroad
547 West Jackson Blvd.
Chicago 6, Illinois

H. F. ENO
Passenger Traffic Manager
Denver & Rio Grande Western Railroad
1531 Stout Street
Denver 1, Colorado

JOSEPH G. WHEELER
Passenger Traffic Manager
Western Pacific Railroad
526 Mission Street
San Francisco 5, California

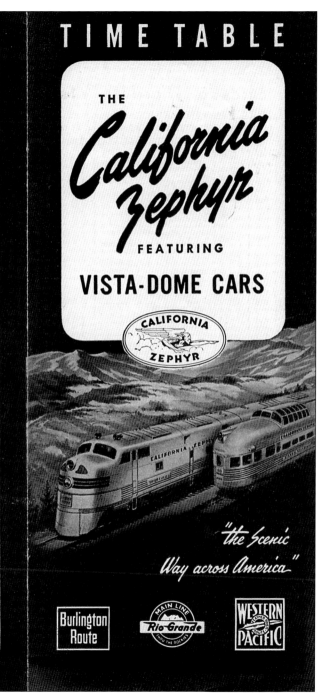

TIME TABLE

THE

California Zephyr

FEATURING

VISTA-DOME CARS

CALIFORNIA ZEPHYR

"the Scenic Way across America"

Burlington Route   Main Line Rio Grande   Western Pacific

California Zephyr public time-table listed arrival and departure times in Chicago and San Francisco (Oakland) for both westbound and eastbound trains. In addition, the back cover contained brief descriptions of the equipment and the front cover slogan "the Scenic Way across America." *Author's collection*

Burlington ran the California Zephyr in joint train operations with Denver & Rio Grande and Western Pacific Railroad. Denver & Rio Grande F3 5524, painted black with yellow stripes and yellow cab nose, fronted the California Zephyr at Glenwood Springs, Colorado, May 21, 1951. *J. M. Gruber collection*

Denver & Rio Grande Alco PA-1 locomotive, painted in the Grande gold-and-silver scheme was photographed at Denver, Colorado. Note the Denver Zephyr neon sign in the background. Date unknown. *J. M. Gruber collection*

California Zephyr-Train 17 (westbound) departed Denver, August 23, 1958, led by Denver & Rio Grande PA-1 locomotive 6003, about to begin its ascent on the Front Range of the Colorado Rockies. *J. M. Gruber collection*

Denver & Rio Grande F3 locomotive 5524 was leading the California Zephyr across Rocky Flats, Colorado. The Flats are famous for strong, hurricane-force winds, June 5, 1962. *J. M. Gruber collection*

Denver & Rio Grande advertisement for passenger train travel on Rio Grande's "Superscenic See-Way." Date unknown. *Author's collection*

The California Zephyr looked terrific with Vista-Domes, as Rio Grande F3 5521 led the train around the curve at Plainview, Colorado, August 9, 1969. *J. M. Gruber collection*

Vista-Dome observation car 882 "Silver Planet" was owned by the Western Pacific Railroad and on August 9, 1969, carried the markers of the California Zephyr at Plainview, Colorado. *J. M. Gruber collection*

Betty Ishell posed for the company photographer in her stylish, two-piece, teal blue Zephyrette uniform aboard a Vista-Dome car. Chicago, Illinois, March 21, 1956. *Courtesy Burlington Northern Santa Fe Railway*

Dining car Luncheon Menu from the California Zephyr: "Grandest train of all," October 1968. *Author's collection*

Luncheon

"As you travel over this bountiful land of ours, may you be ever reminded of the grace Almighty God has bestowed upon us. Let us acknowledge our debt to Him with prayers of thanksgiving."

To insure prompt service write each item on meal check.
"Table Flowers are Colorado Carnations"

(Prices opposite each Entree includes Soup or Juice, Vegetable, Dessert and Beverage)

Soup du Jour   Chilled Grapefruit Juice   Hot Consomme

Filet of Fish, Cole Slaw 2.80
Turkey Fricassee, Buttered Noodles 2.85
Salisbury Steak, Brown Onion Gravy 2.95

Hot Rolls

CHOICE OF TWO

	Carrot Chips	
Whipped Potatoes		String Beans, Butter Sauce
Fruit in Jello	Ice Cream	Peaches in Syrup
Coffee	Hot or Iced Tea	Milk	Decaffeinated Coffee

Sandwich Plates

Hamburger Sandwich on Toasted Bun, Potato Chips, Cole Slaw 2.65
Hot Chicken Sandwich, Whipped Potatoes, Cranberry Jelly 2.80

Ice Cream

Coffee   Hot or Iced Tea   Milk   Decaffeinated Coffee

A la Carte

APPETIZERS   Shrimp Cocktail 1.10   Tomato Juice .40   Soup du Jour .40

ENTREES   Broiled Rib Lamb Chops, French Fried Potatoes 3.85
Sugar Cured Ham and Eggs, Hash Brown Potatoes 2.30
Broiled Sirloin Steak (8 oz.), French Fried Potatoes 3.80
(Includes Bread and Butter)

SANDWICHES   Chicken 1.65   Chicken Salad 1.65   Lettuce, Bacon and Tomato 1.70
(Double Deck)   American Cheese 1.15   Ham 1.80

SALADS   Head Lettuce, Half Portion .50   Lettuce and Tomato 1.35
Chicken Salad, Mayonnaise 2.15
Chilled Fruit Plate, Cottage Cheese 2.25

DESSERTS   Chocolate Sundae .55   Fruit Jello, Whipped Cream .45
Apple Pie .45, ala Mode .70   Sliced Pineapple .50

BEVERAGES   Coffee per pot .35   Tea per pot .35
Hot Chocolate per pot .35   Decaffeinated Coffee per pot .35
Individual Milk .25

Menu
(For children under 12)

A—Fruit Juice, Hamburger Patty, Vegetable, Ice Cream, Milk 1.45
B—Cup of Soup, Ham Sandwich, Potato Chips, Ice Cream, Milk 1.10

Additional charge will be made for service outside the dining car. This service is subject to delay when dining car is busy. Saccharin available upon request.

No. 2-3   Steward in Charge of this Car is ....
No. 1-4   Managers of Dining Car Service
No. 3-6
10/68   *J. W. Vaghy, Burlington, Chicago • L. J. Bernstein, Rio Grande, Denver • W. J. Powell, Western Pacific, Oakland*

Aboard the Vista - Dome

California Zephyr

BURLINGTON • RIO GRANDE • WESTERN PACIFIC

Denver & Rio Grande F3 5541 led the Vista-Dome California Zephyr at Plainview in a scene typical of Colorado and the Rocky Mountains, June 17, 1962. *J. M. Gruber collection*

Western Pacific Railroad was a partner in joint train operations of the California Zephyr from Salt Lake City, Utah, to Oakland, California. Western Pacific F7 804A had the California Zephyr at Oroville, California, January 1, 1968. *J. M. Gruber collection*

Western Pacific Railroad Vista-Dome observation cars 882 "Silver Planet" and sleeper 863 "Silver Mountain." Oakland, California, March, 1970. *Doug Wornom photo*

Burlington Zephyrs arrived and departed from Chicago Union Station, which opened July 23, 1925. Union Station owner railroads included, Pennsylvania, Burlington, Milwaukee Road, and tenant Chicago & Alton. Union Station was designed as two buildings: a Concourse building and the station's colonnade-fronted Head House building (shown), facing the west side of Canal Street. *Author's collection*

Chicago Union Station Concourse building, circa 1925. Located next to the Chicago River, it was connected to the Head House building by an underground passage beneath Canal Street. The Concourse building was razed in 1969. *J. M. Gruber collection*

Burlington shovelnose locomotive and Electro-Motive E-unit teamed up to lead a Vista-Dome Zephyr out of Chicago Union Station. Date unknown. *J. M. Gruber collection*

Burlington Denver Zephyr led by Electro-Motive E5 departed Chicago in August 1949. *Kent Ohlfs collection*

Burlington locomotive E8 9939B departed Chicago on a cold, winter day in 1964 with the Vista-Dome California Zephyr, headed to Oakland, California. *Bob's Photos*

Chicago, Burlington & Quincy passenger extra 9981 West, combined North Coast Limited and Empire Builder charged out of Chicago Union Station in April 1965 for St. Paul, Minnesota. The train was detouring over Milwaukee Road trackage due to the Mississippi River floods. *Bill Raia photo*

Burlington Vista-Dome coach 4730 "Silver Vision" used in Twin Zephyr service. Chicago, Illinois, June 11, 1966. *Owen Leander photo, J. M. Gruber collection*

Burlington dining car 200 "Silver Manor" used on the Kansas City Zephyr. It is shown at the Crooks Terminal Warehouse, which also housed the Burlington Commissary. Chicago, Illinois, date unkown. *J. M. Gruber collection*

Burlington five-compartment, six-double-bedroom sleeping car 454 "Silver Pelican" was part of the second Denver Zephyr (1956) equipment sets. Chicago, Illinois, April 11, 1970. *Owen Leander photo,* J. M. Gruber collection

CB&Q dining car 193 "Silver Café" (used on California Zephyr trains) was parked near the Crooks Terminal Warehouse and Burlington Commissary, April 22, 1971. *Owen Leander photo, J. M. Gruber collection*

Burlington Zephyr with borrowed Great Northern coaches typified the cooperation between Burlington and the parent railroad's Great Northern and Northern Pacific. Highlands, Illinois, June 28, 1970. *Bill Raia collection*

Burlington locomotives led the Great Northern Empire Builder westbound at West Hinsdale, Illinois, August 2, 1958. *Bruce R. Meyer photo*

Great Northern observation car 1291, "St. Nicholas Mountain" at Burlington's 14th Street coach yards in Chicago, July 18, 1962. *J. M. Gruber collection*

Burlington locomotive 9940B highballed a Vista-Dome Zephyr past Berwyn, Illinois on December 29, 1966. *Bill Raia collection, courtesy Kent Ohlfs*

Burlington westbound hotshot freight, led by GP30 locomotive 940 overtook a Burlington commuter train headed to Aurora, Illinois. LaGrange Road, Illinois, June 1965. *Bill Raia collection*

Burlington Northern E9 locomotive 9984 charged out of Chicago Union Station with the Denver Zephyr, prior to Amtrak in April 1971. *Doug Wornom photo*

Burlington Northern 48-seat dining car 201 "Silver Chef" built for the second Denver Zephyrs (1956) departed Chicago, April 1971. Note the chef getting some fresh air before he starts dinner. *Doug Wornom photo*

Burlington Northern E7 locomotive 9924 departed Chicago Union Station with the Denver Zephyr, including Vista-Domes and Burlington Northern pre-merger cars. April 1971. *Doug Wornom photo*

The California Zephyr–Train 18 had just arrived in Chicago with CB&Q Vista-Dome observation car 376 "Silver Penthouse," complete with the California Zephyr tail-sign, September 29, 1962. *Bill Raia collection*

Burlington operated commuter trains from downtown Chicago Union Station to the western suburbs with stainless-steel double-deck cars. Burlington E8 9948B is shown leading a westbound commuter train at Hinsdale, Illinois, July 26, 1969. *Bruce R. Meyer photo*

The famous Burlington Route slogan "Everywhere West" was proudly displayed on the flank of Burlington NW-2 9248 at Eola, Illinois, August 11, 1964. *J. M. Gruber collection*

Sunset on the former Chicago, Burlington & Quincy trackage viewed southwest from Canal Street in Chicago, Illinois, March 1971. The Burlington Zephyrs are now a fallen flag in railroad history. *Doug Wornom photo*

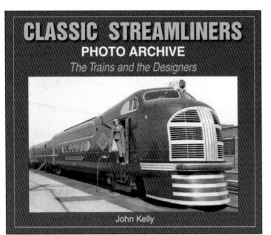
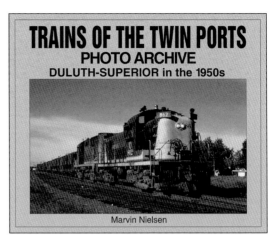
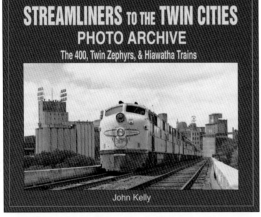
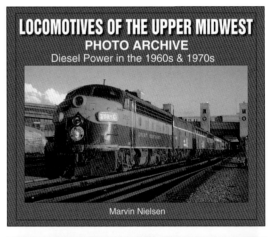
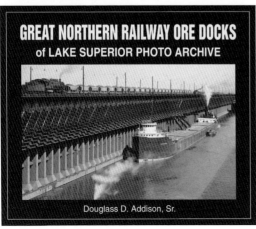